CLASS IS NOW IN SESSION…

Your 21 LinkedIn Questions Answered

Tajuana Ross
"*The LinkedIn Professor*"

Sharon What an excellent client! Thank you Coach Tajuana

thelinkedinprofessor.com
(331)222-9540

Forward

Throughout my years in business, there have been certain people who have left an indelible impression. Tajuana Ross is one of those people. When I first met her, I realized that she was not only a very intelligent and dynamic person, but also gifted in every sense of the word. I found myself enjoying her ideas and her enthusiasm.

Creativity is an important element of success, no matter what your business might be. Tajuana Ross has shown creativity and she knows how to put it into action. Anyone who has been around Tajuana Ross will never forget her or that smile. She is a gifted educator who knows and fully understands her subject.

She loves her business, her passion for her work remains undiminished and as The LinkedIn Professor, she is outstanding.

Dr. Timothy K. Moore

Dedication

To Victoria Ross - for being my inspiration on this journey. I'm not on this mission for my own edification. I do it for those (like you) who are watching my every move. Thank you for being the beautiful soul that you are. If I've been an example of what it looks like to pursue your dreams in spite of your biggest fears, my mission is complete. It brings me immense joy to say that I'm your big sister.

To Scott Carey - if you hadn't nudged me to get on LinkedIn, this monster may not have ever been created. Your sage insight is admirable.

To all of my Coaches - your tireless work on me has pushed me to new heights. I appreciate your dedication to making sure I hit my goals and I'm committed to paying your gifts forward.

To Jeff - you've been my biggest supporter since day one and I love you.

To the Writing Skills teacher who gave me a D+ and told me that my life is one big run-on sentence…thank you. That may have affected my self-esteem then, but I'm a #1 Best Selling Author now. Some of us arrive to the party a little late than others.

And a very special thank you…

To Dr. Chef Timothy Moore - I recall very few phone calls that have changed the trajectory of my life. But September 24th, 2015 is one of those days that I'm incredibly grateful for, because it's the day you told me that I'd be a Best Selling Author by Christmas. I didn't believe you and I told you, "I'm not a writer". But like a great Coach, you walked with me from the birth of the dream to the realization of the dream. And when you called on December 23rd to say, "Congratulations, you're a #1 Best Seller", time stood still. Even though you mentally prepared me for that moment, nothing could get me ready for the physical rush of gratitude and overwhelming joy that I'd experience. The gift you've given me is one that will take a lifetime to properly thank you for.

Table of Contents

The Backstory

My online footprint didn't exist in 2014. I wasn't on Facebook, Twitter, Instagram or any other platform.

Needing to make a change in my work environment, I did what most people do - I applied for jobs on Monster, Career Builder and other sites. What I quickly found was that the opportunities I was looking for weren't the ones I saw online - I wanted to get into the "hidden job market". That required networking. After hitting a brick wall and having my resume end up in the abyss of the online job market, I remembered what a former coworker told me once - "Tajuana, you're a very private person, but you're a professional. You have to be on LinkedIn".

He was right. My professional brand was at stake. And now that it was time to reap the benefits of networking, I didn't have the people I needed in my Rolodex. While I had fostered great business relationships up to that point, I hadn't been strategic in my networking which made my job search more challenging.

During my search, I got a crash course in LinkedIn and learned from those who have been on the platform for years. I attended their webinars, I read their books and I applied what I learned. Sure enough, within 2 1/2 months, I had multiple job offers.

But the bigger takeaway from the time I spent on LinkedIn was that it's more than just a place to find a job. It's a branding tool. I'd even argue that it's the best professional branding tool that exists. So, I set out on a mission to teach its value to those, like me, who had no idea of the message we were sending by not utilizing this tool.

Along the way, I've been asked the same questions repeatedly. This book answers those questions. It's my hope that every reader finds something they can apply immediately in order to leverage their brand on LinkedIn. No matter how bad-ass your Facebook, Twitter or in-person brand is, if you're not visible on LinkedIn, you might want to take copious notes…

1. Why should I be on LinkedIn?

LinkedIn is no longer optional - it's mandatory, if you care about your professional reputation. There are almost half a billion other professionals on the platform and 2 new people join LinkedIn every single second of every single day. If 2 people across the globe join this posse every single day and you're still not active, competing in the emerging "gig economy" will be extremely difficult. LinkedIn is the only place you can go online where you have access to hundreds of millions of people who are specifically there for the purpose of doing business. Because you can't get that anywhere else, your one and only option is to be active on LinkedIn, and that's non-negotiable.

It's been projected that over 40 percent of

the workforce will consist of contractors by 2020. Companies are moving further away from traditional payroll models. You see it happening already with Airbnb, Uber and the surge in ecosystems being built to support the freelancer movement. These companies are hiring individual contributors on a 'project basis'. That model is more profitable because payrolls are costly. People - we're costly. We have demands. We want things like insurance and benefits. How dare we? Companies are now learning that they don't need to pay an employee base anymore to get the job done. There are alternatives to that methodology and the more technology advances, the more options a company has to get the results they need - without the inherent bureaucracy and red tape of payrolls.

If we know that 10 years from now, payrolls will be scarce, then the question becomes, where will the millions of employees who are on payrolls today go in the next 10 years? That's a massive amount of people making an exodus from their environments, virtually all at once...and not always willingly. That means people will have to pivot at a sharp degree. And if they're not already active on a platform like LinkedIn, trying to play catch-up to everybody else will be where a lot of folks get left behind.

Since we're heading in that direction, taking advantage of the one platform that allows us to not only build our professional brand, but to also engage with likeminded professionals from across the globe, seems like an essential component of a successful overall branding strategy.

2. Why does it matter if I'm not on LinkedIn?

I love it when a competitor tells me that they're not on LinkedIn. It gives me a glimpse into their mindset.

When you're not on LinkedIn, you give the general public permission to see you with less professional credibility. LinkedIn is not optional anymore - it's the one place where you're expected to have a presence in order to be taken seriously as a professional. And it's been around long enough for even the Johhny-Come-Lately folks (like me) to have heard about its importance. It doesn't matter what industry you're in or what job you hold - everyone has a personal brand. Unfortunately, too many people don't know what theirs is and by not taking advantage of LinkedIn as a brand strategy tool, they're allowing the rest of the professional world to define it for them…and then they wonder why they don't get the respect, accolades, or opportunities they "deserve".

I picked up on a pattern when listening to the opinions repeated by professionals in different fields across various regions and at multiple levels of business, so I realized that these perceptions are more than just anecdotal. Whether it was said in a private conversation or said publicly, here are the most common conclusions that people came to when they spoke of someone who wasn't on LinkedIn:

- They must not care about their professional image

- They think their job is so safe that they don't need to network with other professionals

- They leave a lot of opportunities on the table

- They must not be social-media-savvy

- They're probably of a certain age

- They don't know how to use LinkedIn

- They can't compete

- We can't do business/partner with them

None of those conclusions are helpful to your mission - especially if they're not true about you.

Mindset is everything and your competitors are judging yours when you say that you're not on LinkedIn. That's counterproductive and hurtful to your professional brand.

3. How is LinkedIn different from Facebook?

Facebook is a social networking platform and LinkedIn is a professional networking platform. Sometimes, people lump LinkedIn into the whole category of social media - and that notion does a disservice to people's perception of LinkedIn. It's not social, it's business. That means the culture is different. That means the discussions are different. The tone is different. The type of content is different. The rules of engagement are different. Because all of that is different, the impact to your overall brand on LinkedIn versus the impact to your brand on Facebook is completely different.

Case in point: It's not shocking for someone to visit a Facebook page and see pictures of last night's shenanigans with libations spread across the table, people chugging those libations and the conga line that ensued. But, people don't expect to see those pictures on LinkedIn (and when they do, it does a number on their perception of you, professionally). Your credibility takes a hit. The professional world doesn't go to LinkedIn for that picture. They go to LinkedIn to consume professional content - articles about business, pictures about something business related, solutions for business problems and making connections with business-minded professionals. Conversely, people go to Facebook to see cat videos. The difference is the mindset. When people understand that, they're more likely to protect their brand reputation and get more strategic about their mission on LinkedIn differently than how they engage random people on Facebook.

4. How do I stand out on LinkedIn?

LinkedIn. Is. Not. A. Glorified. Resume.

The sooner one changes their mindset about its purpose, the sooner one will see the massive impact of networking on LinkedIn.

You distinguish yourself by approaching the platform differently - customize everything.

If you want your profile to look like everyone else's, then follow all of the hyperlinks in LinkedIn that say, "See examples," or, "See what others in your industry are using". If you want to get swallowed up in the ocean of other professionals who do exactly what you do, then that's a 'safe' approach.

However, with the 'never default to the default' mindset, you're forced to think outside the box - how can you deliver your intended message, differently than everyone else? In our culture, people have the attention spans of a mosquito, so you've got to maximize on every opportunity that you have - especially online. Deflecting the mundane will help you stand out.

Your entire LinkedIn profile can be customized as well as repositioned. You have complete control.

Be authentically you. Align your offline brand with your online brand and give us the same you that we would get if we met you at a networking event.

5. Why does my brand matter?

In the new Gig Economy, there is one commandment to live by - "Thou shall monetize thyself or thy shall perish".

Everyone has a professional brand and it matters because it's how the people around you define you - it's your professional reputation and the attributes that you're known for. It's your "Awesome Sauce". It's what makes you different than everyone else. It's what brings out your "swaggeriffic" tendencies. It's what people say (and agree about) when you leave the room. It's what makes you legendary.

Consistently leveraging a professional brand allows you to control how you're perceived by others, connect with the right people and display your thought leadership. All of that positions you to compete at a higher level as the work landscape changes.

Consumers buy from people or companies they know, like and trust. For the public to know, like and trust you, a brand must resonate. Those who intentionally design a strategy around that notion will always attract the right opportunities because they're in the habit of making their impact stick. LinkedIn provides several opportunities to align your strategy with its features.

Just a few ways you can build brand stickiness with your profile:

Customize your public profile URL with your name or brand moniker (i.e. https://www.linkedin.com/in/thelinkedinprof essor). Google loves when you do that and they reward you by bumping you up in their search results over time. You can also add the URL to your email auto-signature and anywhere else you include contact information. The LinkedIn-savvy folks of the world take it as a dead giveaway that you're a novice when your URL is the default series of alphanumeric characters.

Add a background photo to your personal profile that people will recognize as your signature brand marketing (this is different than your profile photo). This banner is one of the first things someone will see when they open your profile, so the visual impact can be lasting. You can change this image periodically to coincide with any major campaigns or product launches.

Create a Kick-Ass Headline that grabs attention. On some pages within LinkedIn, your Headline is the only thing that's displayed other than your name and photo. So, your Headline should compel the reader to want to continue reading - just like the attention-grabbers of a magazine or newspaper article. Unless you change it manually, the last job you had will be auto-populated as your Headline (and there are very few job titles that grab anyone's attention).

Instead of the default Headline, use the opportunity to share your Value Proposition. That way, on a page with several people listed (i.e. a Search Results page), people will have a reason to click on your profile in comparison to the others. That differentiation will help people remember you.

As you compose your Headline, consider that you only have 120 characters to work with - slightly shorter than a Twitter post - so be brief, but specific.

6. Who should I connect with?

Connect with anyone who gives you a mutually beneficial reason to. That could be anyone, but it's important to have relationship building as the overall mission, otherwise it's just collecting numbers in LinkedIn. So, be strategic.

Think of the same people you would seek out at an actual networking event. The people that you would engage with face-to-face, should be who you align with on LinkedIn. The difference is that, now you have access to a much larger number of professionals in that field.

Think outside of the box when you look for commonalities. If you're a Corvette Enthusiast, search for others who share that passion. Then join the appropriate Corvette LinkedIn Groups.

For example, I'm a super nerd. I love to learn and my favorite show ever is Jeopardy. One of the most exciting things to occur on Jeopardy was when Watson competed (I scheduled my vacation around it). Watson is the computer that IBM spent years building - widely perceived to be the smartest machine to ever exist. I've been fascinated with Watson a long time, so of course, I went in search of the brains behind him. Not only did I uncover the people who have invested their time and energy into building him, I found the whole supply chain behind Watson. It takes a lot of businesses to make Watson a reality and that's an ecosystem you could get lost in learning about.

So, connect with people where you see value - and look past the obvious. Business is everywhere.

* My favorite Jeopardy player of all time (other than Watson), is on LinkedIn. That super nerd in me is thrilled to be connected

to them.

7. Do I Need 500 Connections?

Psychologically speaking, there is the perception that anyone wearing the 500+ badge on their profile is "well connected in business". Instinctively, someone's judgment about you is usually one of higher regard and esteem when they see that badge. In the social media world, "Followers" are like digital currency and we've been groomed to be influenced by the size of one's online posse. On the contrary, with only a handful of professional connections after being in a career field for a number of years, someone may judge you negatively - "Well they must be a beginner at what they do if they don't have a lot of people in their professional network" or "They must not be very good at what they do". While their conclusion may or may not actually be true, someone still makes a judgment based on that number. In fact, LinkedIn made sure to drive the behavior of making us care about that number by designing a graphic layout where that number is prominently placed in bold towards the top of every profile. If that number weren't critical to their bottom line metrics, it would buried somewhere at the bottom of the page and it certainly wouldn't be a hyperlink (for 1st level connections). The fact that it's an actual link means that there are algorithms built around that piece of data, which connotes its financial importance.

LinkedIn wants you to "only connect with people you know", so that you can keep your network "small". If they want you to keep your network within those constraints, you can probably guess that it has something to do with their overall business model and their profit goals. LinkedIn makes money off of you if you have a small network - the point of paying them for any of their Premium packages is so that you'll have more access to more features and a larger network of people.

Also birthed in the social media world was FOMO - the fear of missing out. The creators of LinkedIn simply monetized that notion and applied it to the professional crowd.

Think of it this way - the free account gives you a ticket to the dance, but the real party is on the dance floor. LinkedIn's banking on our psychological tendency to crave the dance floor.

But, from a visibility standpoint, the size of your network matters because once you hit 501 connections, your landscape grows exponentially. That additional exposure can be beneficial if the goal is to drive your target audience to your brand. The same goal can be accomplished with a small network - it will just take much longer. Meanwhile, the competitor (who has mastered how to strategically engage their larger network) reaches the goal faster.

Whether the numbers are important or not, LinkedIn is the perfect platform for getting in front of the right people. Quality still matters.

8. Should I accept all of the requests that were sent to me?

You've got an inbox full of connection requests, because you don't know any of the people that sent them. You're skeptical that they might be spammers, competitors or otherwise shady characters, out to steal your connections.

Going to a networking event and only speaking with people you already know is not networking. To get the return on your time invested in attending, one of your goals is probably to meet new people. Well, the same should be true on LinkedIn.

It's ok to be skeptical. If your hunch pans out to be accurate and you run across a few schmucks, LinkedIn provides two great options - hiding that person or deleting them.

Hiding them allows you to keep them in your grand total of connections, without seeing their content. Deleting gets rid of them completely, but of course, your network will shrink.

Your next client might be one of those requests that you've stockpiled. And who knows, you may be the supernatural occurrence that they've been waiting for. It's a mad, mad world out there, but the best networkers are the ones who aren't afraid to meet people - online or off.

9. My competitors want to connect, should I?

Hell yeah.

My friends in sales tell me that they don't want to connect with the competition because they fear that their competitors are going to comb through their connections and find out who they know.

If you've got 500+ connections in your network and you're worried about the few competitors who will actually scroll (or 'troll', depending on your lexicon) through your connections, stop worrying. They are not truly competition if they have that kind of time.

I would cordially invite any of my competitors to spend time looking at who I'm connected to. They'll see that Comedian Chris Rock is my network. So are Motivational Speakers Les Brown and Brian Tracy. So is Kat Cole, the President of FOCUS Brands and Business Mogul Daymond John. But, that tells my competitors absolutely nothing - they still don't know how we're connected. In a hyperconnected world where anyone is a click away, who you're connected to isn't of value anymore, it's how you're connected to them. That can't be determined just by combing through my connections. But, the time it will take my competition to scroll through thousands of people just to learn that is time I want them to take - that gives me hours to get ahead of them while they're distracted.

We all influence a lot of people throughout our lifetime. Surely, we can allow our competitors to have a tiny glimpse into our sphere of influence without it bothering us.

10. Why do I need to personalize my connection requests?

You are hereby forbidden from sending invitations to connect without personalizing them. Forbidden!

Using the default verbiage in your connection request (especially with someone you've never met), is the same as walking up to them, tossing them your business card and quickly walking away without even saying "hello". Who does that?

Instead, start with actually viewing the person's profile (it looks bad when you don't, even if you know them). Once you're finished with the typical content that your eyes gravitate towards, be sure to read what's under "Advice for Contacting". It's customary for the LinkedIn savvy to identify specific information on how they'd like to be engaged.

While you're looking at their profile, take note of things that you share in common, so that you can gauge whether this would really be someone you should connect with. Be choosy - you're only allotted 3,000 connection requests and once you use them all, you've got to go through LinkedIn's approval process to get more.

Personalizing your requests is a way to stand out, since most people don't take the time. It also gives you an opportunity to add context for the person on the receiving end. It doesn't have to be complicated - you only have 300 characters. Your invitation can be as simple as, "Hi. I'm so-and-so. I met you at the such-and-such conference. Your presentation was extremely valuable and I'd love to learn more about your mission to expand into Tokyo. Connect?"

Before I was made aware of the

connecting protocol and understood how important that digital handshake was in shaping perception, I was guilty of sending the generic connection requests. By the third time I got a response saying, " I don't usually accept requests that are not personalized, but...", I stopped that practice. There are plenty of articles written daily about how damaging this is and thank goodness I finally gave it credence. The quality of the relationships built after making the shift was not only apparent, but also revenue generating in the long run.

* In the event that you happen to send a connection request without personalizing it, IMMEDIATELY send a message, apologizing for your gaffe. Be sure to include whatever verbiage you would've sent in the first place.

11. How important is your profile picture?

Your LinkedIn profile picture can make you or break you.

Our brains are wired to see a picture and judge whether a person is competent and trustworthy within a nanosecond. And since our future paying clients, investors, partners and bosses are eyeing us, it makes sense to put our best foot forward. We can't help that people will make career impacting judgments about us, but we can certainly make an effort to mitigate the risk of having the wrong judgments made. Nothing makes someone recoil like the wrong LinkedIn profile picture - it holds more weight than any Facebook picture you post. In many cases, it's the very first time someone sees you.

Networking requires human interaction. On LinkedIn, that interaction begins with a professionally done headshot. If you plan on competing in any segment of business and protecting your overall brand, make the investment to set yourself apart from the crowd.

We've all seen the profile pictures that just don't work - the ones that have:

- Babies with adorable and pinchable cheeks. Cute, but that's a Facebook picture, not LinkedIn.

- You at the baseball game. Who cares that you nabbed nosebleed seats? We also can't tell which one is you.

- You in your tux - yeah, we can tell that was your wedding day - by the looks of the good time you're having, we're left to wonder if that's the only time you've ever worn a tux.

- You in your wedding dress. Oh, c'mon.

- The husband and wife team - just our luck, your name is Chris or Pat or Kelly or…

- "The Hanging Chad" - no really, the guy who was clearly cut out of your picture is named Chad. We know that because even though his body is cut out of the picture, he had his arm around your shoulder and we can still see the "Chad" tattoo on his wrist. Couldn't Photoshop that out, eh?

- You at the bar (or any other fine establishment serving libations). Hey, is that Chad in the background???

- The Duck Face or the bathroom mirror selfie. No explanation needed.

- Your company logo. The eyes are

the window to the soul and your eyes...well, they're the perfect RGB. But, remember - people want to do business with people they know, like and trust - not faceless logos.

- No picture at all. With no picture at all, you've given the general public permission to come to any conclusion they please...which is never in your favor. This is especially true when they can go to Facebook and see plenty of your (unprofessional) pictures.

Do yourself a favor - put more thought into your brand strategy if your profile picture falls into any of these categories.

12. Should I write in the first or third person?

In his Bigger and Blacker stand-up routine, Chris Rock said "When you meet somebody for the first time, you're not meeting them - you're meeting their representative!"

Even though he was speaking of dating, that's exactly what comes to mind when I see someone's profile written in the third person. It's as though the their 'people' wrote it for them and you're meeting their representative. It certainly doesn't conjure up "have a business conversation with me".

People go to LinkedIn because they want to build professional relationships. Relationships are built on one's ability to connect directly with you. Third person doesn't lend itself to that.

While there was an era when speaking in the third person would impart humility, over time, it became synonymous with being conceited.

The content in your Summary should be written in the first person, as though you're telling your story. The reader should feel like you're right next to them. You can't get that result when you write in the third person.

(Re)write your story in first person (you've got a maximum of 2,000 characters) and watch what happens to the quality of your LinkedIn interactions. Leave the third person speak for more formal occasions.

13. I have more than one job. Do I need multiple profiles?

Nope. Your LinkedIn profile is the digital equivalent of a super model's portfolio. If you've ever watched a super model in the heart of New York City, you would've seen them walking around town with a big portfolio binder (before the dawn of tablets). Inside of that book are all of the pictures that they've taken - headshots, action shots, beauty shots, commercial shots, etc...

Your LinkedIn profile is a one-stop shop for someone to see the entirety of all things you - pertinent to your professional career. Nobody is a one-trick-pony anymore, so it's ok to show off your diverse work life. While it's not necessary to tell us what you were doing in 1982, we should be able to leave your profile with a robust view of your past, present and future. That means, how did you get to this point? Where are you now and what are you working on? What's the next project for you?

When you separate all of your roles and create multiple profiles, it's confusing to the rest of the world. Which one should we connect with? Which one should we endorse your skills on? Which one should we give you a recommendation on? Which one will you see our messages on? Which one do you actually know the password for?

Don't make us guess. We'll probably guess incorrectly - if we guess at all.

14. Do I Need 50 Skills Listed For Endorsements?

Any random 50 skills, no. Your professional image is worth a little more effort than that.

Even though your skills are sprinkled into the content throughout the Summary and Experience sections of your profile, the Skills section gives your connections an opportunity to vouch for your skills, by endorsing you. It's a great way to foster relationships.

But, it's also a great way of widening your LinkedIn footprint. Each one of the skills listed is clickable. When you click them, you are directed to a Search Results page that shows other professionals with that same skill. Those are people you already have something in common with.

More importantly though, if someone does a search for a particular skill that you have on your profile, you will show up in the search results. So, if you only have a few skills listed, you limit your exposure and your chance to be found. The maximum amount of skills that LinkedIn allows is 50 - that's 50 opportunities to be found - just on LinkedIn alone.

Most people don't realize that LinkedIn and Google are BFFs (Best Friends Forever). One way to take advantage of that relationship is by giving Google more opportunities to match your face and your name with your professional skills, via your LinkedIn profile.

I did a random search once for a Toastmasters meeting in my area once. To my surprise, my LinkedIn profile appeared on the first page of the results. That was before I understood how the magic of the Google and LinkedIn union worked, if given the opportunity.

Since you probably have important keywords elsewhere throughout your profile, the Skills section can be used to paint a more of well-rounded view of you. There's room here for creativity and a peek into your personality, when you go beyond the standard regurgitation of your resume bullet points. The reader will gain more insight into who you are, which opens the door to more of a well rounded business conversation.

15. I Have A Profile, Now What?

Congratulations, you have a LinkedIn profile - so do more than 400 million other people.

The real power behind the platform, though, is when you're not just on it, but you're active on it. Your profile was just the first step - now you're at the party, but you're still not on the dance floor. In order to get on the dance floor and actually dance, you've got to have more than just that profile.

Before you jump right in though, sit back and watch - observe the culture first. LinkedIn is not Facebook, so you can't just complete a couple of word search games or math problems and think you've arrived - in fact, completing word search games or math problems would get you blackballed in certain circles. Instead, exert energy in positioning yourself as a relevant resource, serve others, and build key relationships where there is mutual value.

It helps to have a plan to engage as you begin to connect with the right people. But when you find them, take it a step further and extend your online relationship to an offline environment. Make time to interact with the people in your network. When I connect with people I've never met, I like to invite them to 'virtual coffee' or to the local coffeehouse, if they're in the area. They're usually taken aback because they're not used to a stranger wanting to engage them. But, the point of networking is to learn something about the other person and how you can help them - to do that, you should at least be open to having a conversation with someone that you may not know well.

* Disclaimer: Approach networking on

LinkedIn like you would dating. It's a parallel process. So, before you go filling your calendar with random possible-ax-murderers, do the digital equivalent of "scoping out the bar". Survey the landscape first.

A few other things you can do, now that you have a profile:

•   Pick a few groups to be active in. You may be a member of several, but dedicate time to actually participating only in a few. Depending on the group's value, you can rotate quarterly to widen your reach.

•   Decide on a schedule and share pertinent content that your network would find beneficial (whether it's your own content or curated). You should also make it a habit to comment on other posts - keeping in mind that your words will be out there forever. The context that you add will help your network - over time - get to know you. When your network begins to habitually see your value, they start to look forward to your content because they know they'll gain priceless insight.

- When LinkedIn prompts you with the update about so-and-so's new job, congratulate them. People love being acknowledged and to network purposefully means that you've got to put in the work. But remember - add value. Take the time to say something thoughtful in your comment, though, instead of the generic auto-populated "Congrats" greeting. Your relationship with that person will be strengthened, which goes a long way in business. Just proceed with caution in case someone is simply updating their profile and forgot to go into 'stealth mode' - you'll raise a few eyebrows if you're congratulating them for getting a job they've had for years. Since, I've made that mistake enough times, I now open the person's profile first to verify that they did indeed start a new job before I congratulate them.

- Give endorsements (no matter how silly people think they are). It's just good career karma because what goes around, comes around and they do matter, if used wisely. You can give up to 150 a day and it's a great tool when you need to reengage someone that you haven't been in touch with in a while. It's also a healthy practice to actually thank people when they give you more than a few endorsements at a time (that means that they weren't prompted by some random LinkedIn pop-up window encouraging them to endorse you). Unless you've changed your communication settings, you'll see an email confirmation when you receive these pats on the back, so you'll always know who to follow up with. Furthermore, when I see someone who doesn't list pertinent skills that I know they have, I'll add new ones so that they can be found for those attributes. Doing that usually leads to a conversation where someone tells me that they didn't even know that was possible. So, now they've given me an opportunity to teach and add value…is that kind of result silly?

16. I Created A Profile Last Year. Why Do I Need To Update It?

A year is a long time - a lot of things can happen in a year. Businesses revisit their objectives on a continuous basis, with benchmarks set along the way to ensure that they hit their metrics. So, if your branding strategy is parallel to your overall business goals, your LinkedIn profile becomes the perfect place to show off that progress.

When you add content as events happen, it won't seem so daunting. LinkedIn is not a "set-it-and-forget-it" tool, so if a year has gone by since you've updated your profile, you probably have a branding dilemma. When you use LinkedIn more fluidly, your results will better reflect your professional life.

When you get stuck on what to add, go back to your calendar. If you've managed it effectively, then you'll be able to quickly recap the events that are worth capturing on your profile. You want to look for things like media, key presentations, press releases, client feedback, new partnerships and any other content that paints the full picture of your wins.

In addition to adding content, it's a good idea to prune sometimes. When there are things that no longer align with your overall mission or your brand, it's ok to remove them. Just make sure that as you remove content, the remaining verbiage still flows for the reader.

When your profile looks stale, it affects people's perception of you. It makes it obvious that you're not active on LinkedIn and that's never a good look.

* Go to Account Settings and select "Turn on/off your activity broadcasts" under Privacy Controls if you're making several

adjustments. Otherwise, you annoy your network when you clog their home page with the notifications of your tweaks.

17. Can I Sell My Widgets On LinkedIn?

Salespeople who have the tendency to push a spiel in person, will have the tendency to do so on LinkedIn as well. "Social Selling" is still selling and it's still a process. But, when people skip the networking activities and go straight for the selling activities, they're not all that successful. The networking piece is even more critical in the digital world.

At the typical networking event, you usually have a chance to introduce yourself and give your 'elevator pitch'. You probably wouldn't do a full product demonstration and if you tried, it probably wouldn't be received well because it's not the proper forum for that. It's the same thing on LinkedIn. Granted, you may end up getting sales as a result of the event, but you have to network first.

We've all accepted a connection request on LinkedIn from a stranger who immediately turned around and sent us a message with their sales pitch in it (without even looking at our profile to see if we were the ideal client). The message was canned verbiage with the generic salutation, "Hi" and they barfed up every link to their product sites (which we'll never click out of spite). Even if your kind heart prevented you from promptly deleting them, the experience probably left a bad taste in your mouth. Yet, if they had mirrored their offline sales process with their approach on LinkedIn, they'd net a higher conversion rate - and maintain a positive brand image.

LinkedIn is a networking platform where you'll make sales as a result of your networking skills. It might be tempting, but don't put the cart before the horse.

18. Why Should I Write On LinkedIn's Publishing Platform?

For starters, it's free. Publishing on LinkedIn does not cost you a dime and you don't have to be a premium member. Because there's no cap on how much content you can create, you can write as much as you want (as long as it's relevant to your brand, of course). If you wanted to publish an article every day, you could. Unlike other sites, you still own your content when it's published on LinkedIn.

Secondly - that Google/LinkedIn BFF thing. They never go anywhere without each other. So, when you publish an article on LinkedIn, Google sees it and deposits that currency to your digital bank account.

The real benefit, though, is that your target audience gets a glimpse into your thought process, how you stack up against your competitors and your way of doing business. It's exposure that you may not be getting on your blog or your website that can concrete your credibility. It's also digital currency that can be repurposed to expand your online footprint. And since the Publishing Dashboard provides detailed engagement metrics, you can really drill deep into building a network of like-minded people.

19. What Should I Write About On LinkedIn's Publishing Platform?

It's important to not look at the publishing platform as somewhere that only writers can thrive. We are all writers - some of us just take longer to get the words out of our heads than others.

If you're using your authentic voice and you don't have trepidation about sharing your opinion, the publishing platform should be a component of your branding strategy. In addition to helping you stand out on LinkedIn, writing articles (LinkedIn calls them long-form posts) will boost your standing in Google's search results. Don't forget, Google and LinkedIn are BFFs.

So, write about what's happening in your industry, your specific segment of business and even what you see happening in your own office. Write about your experiences, the lessons you were able to apply and their results. Write about your mistakes, so people can learn from them. Be open to the discussion that occurs as a result of controversy. Not everyone will agree with your point of view, but the engagement that comes out of lively debate helps us all learn, so there's no reason to avoid it.

* Just be sure to have someone else proofread your work before you post your articles. Don't trust your own eyes to proofread. It's worth the extra time, otherwise your typo-ridden articles will be counterproductive and they'll end up hurting your brand.

20. Why Isn't LinkedIn Working For Me?

LinkedIn is not a passive tool. LinkedIn requires consistent activity in order to stand out, which means you have to invest time into it. Building a brand isn't something you do overnight and building that brand on LinkedIn has to be strategic.

Where most people go wrong is treating their LinkedIn profile like their online resume, instead of a branding tool. They offer no value and their profile looks like everyone else's. While that may be enough for some, others have figured out that LinkedIn pays dividends when they learn how to differentiate themselves and engage their network.

LinkedIn offers a variety of metrics that allow you to track how well you're utilizing the platform. For example, you can check your SSI (Social Selling Index), which is the LinkedIn equivalent of your Klout Score. That tool suggests ways to establish your professional brand, find the right people, share relevant insight and grow your network.

You can also monitor the response rate of your activity, going back 30 days, which gives you plenty of time to examine your network's engagement patterns and adjust accordingly.

If you're not getting results on LinkedIn, chances are you don't have a strategy in place...but, your competitors do.

21. What's The Biggest LinkedIn Mistake?

Saying the words, "I'm not on LinkedIn" out loud causes your competitors all over the globe to erupt in simultaneous and thunderous applause. That's one less 'professional' to compete with. And by the time you catch up, it'll be too late.

As someone who was adamant about keeping a tiny online footprint, I understand someone's hesitation about putting themselves out there into cyberspace, for all to see…for an eternity. But, let's face it, social media is here to stay and out of all the options for professionals, LinkedIn is the one that's critical in your branding blueprint. It's the one that can instantly ruin your professional reputation when you don't take it seriously. It's the one that can impact your revenue or your income. It's the one that you can't afford to ignore.

About The Author

Entrepreneurs and Wantrepreneurs hire Tajuana Ross when they're stuck. She's the President/CEO of **Get Over Yourself Career and Life Coaching, Inc.**, #1 Best Selling Author of **Class Is Now In Session - Your 21 LinkedIn Questions Answered**, Host of the Podcast **The LinkedIn Professor - Schooling You on Building and Engaging Your Network**, Host of the Radio Show **I Call Bullshit - Remix Your Negative Self-Talk**, Creator of **The LinkedIn Mastermind** Academy, an award winning Professional Speaker and Celebrity LinkedIn Ghostwriter.

Tajuana's background as a former Corporate Rat-Racer includes more than 10 years in Sales and 15 years as a Sales Training Professional with companies like MCI WorldCom, AT&T and Verizon

Wireless. Now a Certified Facilitator, Certified Professional Life Coach and Certified Social Branding Coach, Tajuana uses her business acumen and access to wide-reaching platforms to lead people towards monetizing their professional brand in the emerging 'Gig Economy'. Known for her candid cadence, Tajuana brings unfiltered real-life stories to her interactions as a way to connect with her tribe.

Friends know Tajuana as "The LinkedIn Professor", "The Bullshit Remixer" and she's been dubbed "The Harriet Tubman of Corporate America" for the number of people that she's coached on their journey from payroll to purpose. You'll catch her wearing her signature "Blazer and Chucks", as she's empowering business people everywhere to get unstuck.

"Happy Linking."

- Tajuana Ross

For more information, visit:
www.thelinkedinprofessor.com

For Bulk Orders and Speaking Engagements, call (331)222-9540 or Email:
tajuana@thelinkedinprofessor.com.

Send a Personalized Connection Request on LinkedIn:
www.linkedin.com/in/thelinkedinprofessor

Made in the USA
Columbia, SC
18 September 2019